Former PGA Golf Professional and *USA Today* bestselling author Dean Wesley Smith walks you step-by-step, club-by-club from your car to the first tee and beyond in a laugh-out-loud style that not only teaches, but entertains.

Also by

Dean Wesley Smith

The Poker Boy Universe:

Novels

Slots of Saturn

Short Stories

The Old Girlfriend of Doom
Dead Even
Gambling Hell
Luck Be A Lady
Sighed the Snake
The Smoke That Doesn't Bark
The War of Poker
Fighting the Fuzzy-Wuzzy
Nonexistent No More
Daddy is an Undertaker
Pink Shoes and Hot Chocolate
Shootout in the Okey-Doke Casino
Dried Up
The Empty Mummy Murders
Living Time
Not Saleable For Sale
Just Shoot Me Now!
For the Balance of a Heart

the First Tee Panic

AND OTHER VERY REAL GOLF STORIES

DEAN WESLEY SMITH

WMG PUBLISHING

The First Tee Panic

Published 2014 by WMG Publishing
www.wmgpublishing.com
Cover art copyright © Julien Tromeur/Dreamstime,
Andres Rodriguez/Dreamstime
Interior art copyright © Julien Tromeur/Dreamstime
Book and cover design copyright © 2014 WMG Publishing
Cover design by Allyson Longueira/WMG Publishing
ISBN-13: 978-0-615-93529-4
ISBN-10: 0-615-93529-X

*First published in slightly different form in Smith's Monthly 1, 2 and 3,
October, November, December 2013*

Contents

the First Tee Panic

AND OTHER VERY REAL GOLF STORIES

1

HELP! I DON'T WANT TO WHIFF THE FIRST SHOT

IT'S A HORRID NIGHTMARE. For some reason, I have it just about every time I play in a golf tournament, or have a big game lined up with friends or other professional golfers. I've heard that other golfers have nightmares like it, but no one seems to deal with the dreams and the nightmares that come along with the game. I'm not going to either, but I am going to talk about what causes my nightmare.

The first tee shot. (Sound effects here of those four words bouncing around in a massive echo chamber, then fading into the distance like a bad horror movie.)

My nightmare goes like this: I'm standing on the first tee, the morning sun is just breaking over the rocks and cactus of the Scottsdale desert. The dew is still thick in the heavy rough, but the fairway is a green, freshly mowed road stretching impossibly narrow in front of me.

In the nightmare, I always feel great, muscles loose, mind focused, hands warm. My three golfing companions have all hit their first tee shots, all perfectly down the middle of the fairway, and they are now waiting for me.

The group behind us has arrived at the tee and are sitting in their carts also waiting.

Here goes. I step to my ball, take a mighty swing...

...and miss.

A clean whiff. A fly could have made a larger impact on that ball by simply landing on it. Not even the wind of my club passing shook it.

My *Titleist 1* ball with the "1" underlined stares up at me.

Suddenly, I'm sweating in the cool morning air. My playing companions are snickering, two guys in the group behind us are shaking their heads, the other two are trying unsuccessfully to not laugh.

I try to laugh with them. I make a lame joke about a practice swing, take my stance again, another mighty swing, and another clean miss.

It's as if the ball isn't where it's supposed to be.

I've been playing the game of golf since I was three, been a professional for decades. Yet there sits the ball.

Titleist 1 mocks me.

My friends are sitting in the carts, laughing, making ugly snorting noises. The players in the group behind are laughing so hard, one of them falls to the cart path. Even the starter is laughing.

It is *not* funny. Trust me.

I swing again.

Miss.

Again I swing, this time even harder and faster.

Another miss.

I can barely breathe. My arms feel trapped, pinned against my side. I go to kick the ball, but my feet won't move. The wonderful day of golf has turned into a swirling, sweating nightmare of laugher and humiliation.

Then, thankfully, right at that point, I always wake up. Usually, I've twisted the sheets into a tight mess around myself, pinning my sweating body to the bed in a pile of sheet knots that would earn a Boy Scout a merit badge. After I get untangled, I glance at the clock. It's usually about ten minutes before the alarm is supposed to go off.

Ten minutes before I'm supposed to start getting ready for a beautiful day of golf. A beautiful day, that is, if I can manage to get off that first tee.

Now, understand, this dream doesn't come from any real event. No, my imagination has done this all by itself. Not once, not ever, have I whiffed a golf ball on a first tee, yet that reality doesn't help kill the fear. The little voice, deep in the back of my head whispers, "There could always be a first time."

Am I the only golfer who has this type of nightmare, these kind of waking fears? Nope. Almost every golfer I've ever talked to has something like it. And almost without exception, every golfer has a deep fear of the first shot on the first tee, even if they don't have nightmares that twist sheets into rags.

Think about how many times you have heard a touring professional golfer talking to an announcer on television. The conversation always goes something like this:

Announcer: "*How was your round?*"

Professional tour golfer: "*Once I got off the first tee and got settled down, I played pretty well.*"

The first tee scares the hell out of touring professionals. Trust me, the last thing those players on the big tours want is to roll their tee shot along the ground in front of a million people on national television. They think about it, have nightmares about it.

Yet it never happens.

Why? Because they also know how to deal with the fear, how to make sure they don't send a ball bouncing down the fairway to stop close enough to the tee that the television networks don't even have to change a camera position.

The pros and better golfers have methods of getting ready for that first shot, little ways of making sure they at least make contact with the ball. I'm going to detail out some of these methods, these tricks of the game, right from the moment you get out of the car to the mighty first swing.

Step by step, I'll get you from the bag drop and safely off the first tee. Trust me, it can be done without a nightmare of humiliation, just like the professional golfers manage it.

I might not be able to help you hit the fairway, but sometimes the goal of the first tee isn't to hit it straight, but to simply get the ball in the air and as far away from you as you can manage. Second shots are a whole lot easier if you're still not standing on the tee box.

Trust me on that as well.

2

HELP! WHAT DO I DO WHILE A BAG BOY UNLOADS MY CLUBS

MAKING SURE YOU make contact with the ball on the first tee actually starts when you arrive at the golf course.

Golf is a mental game. Keep repeating that.

Golf is a mental game.

To safely get that big driver's club face on that tiny little white ball on the first tee, you have to start thinking like a golfer. From the parking lot to the bar after the round, you're a golfer. The day job is gone, the family and all the chores around the house are forgotten completely. You arrive at the course, ready for a great day of golf.

So getting ready, getting yourself in the right state of mind is important right from moment one. And that moment is when the bag boy is unloading your clubs from the trunk of your car.

I'm assuming a big golf game on a big country club, on golf courses that cover deserts like those around Phoenix or Palm Springs, or beautiful tracks that wind through pine-tree-covered hillsides like those in Sun Valley or outside of Chicago or New York.

You're a golfer, a privileged member of the working class. You've bought the most expensive clubs, got new head-covers for your birthday from your kids, practiced after work and on weekends. You even make empty handed practice swings while in elevators and in front of mirrors. You're ready, you've carved out the time, and you've finally driven or flown a great distance to a top golf course. You have the right to be there, you've paid for it, and you don't want it spoiled by any first tee missteps, so start thinking like a golfer as you enter the gates of the club.

If you're like most of us and are used to just grabbing your sticks from your trunk or your locker at your local muni course, the first thing you're going to notice different about these big golf resorts and country clubs is a sign as you drive up the landscaped driveway.

Bag Drop.

If you've never, ever been to one of these types of golf courses, just follow the sign's arrows and stop your car when you see some well-dressed, smiling young man or woman approach as if they know what they are doing. This is not where you will park, but it is the first step in getting to the course.

Sometimes, this bag person is the lowest assistant professional at the course, but more often he or she is just a college student who loves golf. Either way, their job is to greet you with a friendly smile, make note of your arrival through some hidden and high-tech communications system, get your clubs out of your car and put them on a cart.

Don't even think about walking the course and carrying your own bag. These top courses won't allow it. The cart fee is required and is part of the massive amount of money you're going to pay when you reach the pro shop.

A small tip of a few dollars to the bag person is in order, combined with a thank you and a respectful attitude if you hope to see your clubs again before the round starts.

One side note about timing. For years I played socially with a group of other top golfers. We would often go to Phoenix and Scottsdale to play golf in the dead of winter. Our goal while there was to play as much as possible, so we often had the earliest tee time allowed by any golf course. This bag boy stuff works fine and dandy for anyone scheduled at a moderate time after sunrise. I can't tell you how many times I headed down a first fairway and the sun was just pretending to light the sky, let alone peak over the nearest cactus. Bag boys don't exist at that hour and don't expect them to be there.

Also, let me say that playing golf before the sun comes up just isn't fun most of the time and should be left to only the extreme golf fanatics. If you do tee off before sunrise regularly, seek help.

So, what do you do to get ready for that first big shot on the first tee as the bag boy unloads your bag from the trunk of your car, cleans your already well-cleaned clubs, and straps them to the back of a cart?

You could stand there staring. Or sit in your car waiting for the trunk to close, listening to the morning news. Or you could use the time to do something you're going to have to do first thing anyway.

Put on your golf shoes.

There is no reason to carry a pair of shoes down into a club house locker room, then store your street shoes in some corner or in the cart while you play. Your time before the round is better served in other areas of preparation. So, while the bag boy is doing his or her thing with your expensive golf clubs, sit in the open door of your car and put on your golf shoes.

But one warning. You still have to drive your car to the parking lot. Diving with your golf spikes on can get tricky. I don't think the Federal Transportation Board has any figures on exactly how many car accidents are caused by wearing golf shoes while driving, but I would wager the number is pretty high. And we won't mention that little dent in that Porsche at the Palm Springs Country Club back in 1973. I left a note before I went out to play.

Honest.

3

HELP! HOW DO I ACT LIKE A REAL GOLFER IN THE PRO SHOP?

AT THESE BIG COUNTRY CLUBS, the pro shops are major businesses, large rooms filled with a massive number of golfing attire, bags, clubs, and balls. The main desk is usually a beautiful, wood-carved monster of a counter that three or four people can fit behind without even touching. It's usually elevated so that the professionals behind it look *down* at the customers.

Or so it seems to me. Maybe I just slouch every time I go into a major pro shop. The places, for some reason, are just not that comfortable, and I've spent my share of years working in them, standing behind those elevated counters. The problem is, the last thing any of us need in our quest to get the ball airborne off the first tee is added nervousness caused by the giant, looming monster of the pro shop.

But you can't avoid the place. The pro shop is like the narrow part of an hourglass, with the outside world filtering down through the pro shop to emerge out on the golf course. Luckily, on the way back to the real world, you don't have to make a return voyage through the pro shop. The bar, maybe, but not the pro shop.

So, let me suggest a routine to get you safely through the pro shop and outside again into the crisp morning air.

First off, find the right entrance.

Sounds simple, right? Nope, often this is a lot harder than it sounds. These big country clubs have *Members Only* areas and really fancy restaurants with tiny little signs warning you and your golf shoes away. Problem is, those little signs are so small, the only way you're going to see them is if you know they are there. I've missed many of those signs and ended up in a swank dining room, on expensive carpet that was never meant to see a golf spike.

Trust me, making this kind of wrong-turn-blunder can really set you back, especially when some waiter has to lead you firmly, but oh-so-politely back the way you came.

Once you are safely in the pro shop, the first thing you want to do is pick up a putter out of the two hundred putters lined up along the wall on a rack. Pretend to be considering buying it by making a few pretend putts.

For heaven's sake, never hit a ball in these practice putts, even though there will be some hanging around a practice ball return. Banging a ball off a display case and under a rack of woman's blouses is not the way you want to start your day. The thought of that kind of putt will haunt you on the third green.

Just pretend putting. Got that? Act cool.

Of course, you have no intention of spending five hundred bucks on a new putter right before a big round when your old twenty-six dollar yard-sale-special is working just fine. But pick one up and look at it seriously anyway.

Next, find the ugliest putter in the bunch, the one with a club head bigger than a toaster, and make a joke about it to the nearest person.

That person will always respond with a joke in kind, unless you happen to be talking to the representative for the putter company. Early in the morning, there is little chance of that happening.

After a few laughs, head directly for the counter to check in and pay for your upcoming round. While there, spending the big bucks on the green fees and cart rental, go ahead and buy a sleeve of golf balls with the club's name on them. Yes, I know you brought enough golf balls along in your bag. These new balls are only for emergencies and if not used, take them home as a reminder of your great day and how much you spent for one round of golf. Sort of like a Disneyland set of Mickey Mouse Ears, only you don't have to wear the golf balls.

Don't ask the pro what kind of balls are the best. Just buy *Titleist* or the new *Nike* ball because Tiger uses them. The country club will have their logo on either type.

And when you ask for the balls, ask for an exact brand. For example, say, "Oh, and give me a sleeve of the *Titleist Professionals*." Or whatever they are called these days. Don't say, "Give me the gold pack." Not golfing cool and might get you looked-down-upon by the professional even more.

Then, and this is critical, ask about practice balls, or participate in a conversation another player is having with the professional about practice balls. The pro will tell you how to get them and where the range is at that point.

Thank him or her, but never tip them. I saw one man in California try to tip a golf professional in his golf shop and I thought the professional was going to take a driver to the side of the guy's head. You tip bag boys, cart boys, waiters, and bartenders. Never golf professionals, unless they give you a really good lesson on the driving range that you have already paid a bunch of money for. Then just add in a little extra.

But never in the pro shop.

So, you have paid, you have the knowledge of where to get the practice balls. Mission accomplished.

Now, without another look at the putters or drivers or six thousand sand and flop wedges, head for the door with a sure stride of a person with purpose.

You're going to go hit practice balls.

Repeat that thought in a very deep-voiced way. *You're going to go hit practice balls.*

Practice in golf is a very serious thing, especially right before an important round, so act the part. It's time to go to work, to get ready to get that first shot off the first tee and into the air.

Just make sure you take your new sleeve of recently purchased golf balls with you as you leave the pro shop. Turning around and going back to get them can really break a serious practice mood.

4

HELP! WHICH CLUB SHOULD I HIT FIRST ON THE DIVING RANGE?

YOU'VE FOUND THE MASSIVE open green expanse of the hitting area of the driving range, parked your cart along the edge of the concrete path, and have gone around to the back of the cart to your bag to get a club.

But which club to hit first?

You have fourteen clubs to choose from. If you have more than fourteen, maybe from your kids tossing extras in, make sure to take them out before you get to the first tee. Rule is, only fourteen clubs allowed. And actually, at the moment you only have thirteen to pick from. You're not going to be hitting any balls with your putter on the driving range. And if you even think about it, you made the wrong turn at the front driveway. You wanted the course with the castles and the big clown mouth that opens and closes.

So, thirteen clubs to pick from.

But which one first?

You glance around at the others hitting balls, sending those clean white spheres into the air with a sense of beauty and purpose you only can hope for. There doesn't seem to be any logic in what clubs they are using, since they arrived at different times before you. Some are hitting drivers, others flip wedges, others long irons.

Don't panic, there is a real reason for starting with certain clubs first in a warm-up practice session. And if you follow the basic guidelines I'm about to give you, not only will your warm-up be good for your body, but it will help you get off that dreaded first tee.

First, grab a seven iron.

Your goal with this club is to just get your body lose enough to swing a golf club. You have no intention of hitting good shots right off the bat, so don't even think about it. Just take the seven iron to the teeing area nearest your cart, do a few basic warm-up stretches to get muscles loosened, then generally hit a ball with about a half swing.

Half swing means the club doesn't go above head high on the back swing.

This going slow on the first swing is so that you don't pull tired and car-weary muscles. Last thing you need on this special day of golf is to be hauled off in an ambulance with a wrenched back. And trust me, I've seen it happen more than once from these first swings.

Let me repeat, you don't care if you hit the shot right or not. Don't even look. Just half-swing and make contact.

That's success at this time of the morning.

Take another half swing and hit another. Then on the third take a little fuller swing. Repeat this for five to ten balls until your hands can feel the club, your grip doesn't feel like you're holding the head of an alien snake, and your back stops cracking.

If you are going to be the very first group off the tee, the grass is still damp with dew, and you have on two sweaters and a thick windbreaker, make this first part of the practice at least twenty golf balls, or until your hands stop stinging every time you hit the ball.

Now, you're a little looser and warmed up, so go back to the cart and get a nine iron.

It's time to start hitting shots directly at a target.

Golf is, after all, a game of targets.

Never hit a golf shot after the first ten or so warm-up balls without a target clearly in mind. If you can actually keep a target in mind for every shot of the round, you will cut strokes off your game. But that lesson is for another time. Right now you are practicing to get off the first tee, and picking a target is critical.

There should be signs on the driving range in front of you, or different colored flag poles stuck into pretend greens. Those are targets. Pick the one that says 100 Yards and aim at it. With about a three quarter swing with the nine iron, fire away.

Five or ten balls, you should be narrowing in or over that sign, and if you're pretty strong, maybe even bouncing the nine irons in front of the 150 yard sign.

But don't push, don't try to hit anything hard. Work on just making smooth, comfortable swings, time after time, repeating the same swing over and over and over.

After being a game of targets, golf is secondly a game of repeating an impossible movement of your body. It is a very physical game, so don't ignore that aspect. You are warming up now to have a great, injury-free day, and get that first shot off the first tee.

Go easy.

Another tip: Step away from the ball between every shot. Don't just pull another ball to you and fire away. Put another ball in place and then step back, as if this next shot is your first shot on the course. Pick a target and just repeat the word *smooth* over and over.

If you don't understand what I mean by smooth, just think about Fred Couples' golf swing. It don't get no smoother than that.

Now after ten balls or so with the nine iron, get a five iron, pick a target just beyond the 150 yard sign and do another ten balls, again working on staying smooth. Just like the nine iron, make sure you step away from the ball between each shot, line up a target, swing smooth.

If you miss a shot, forget it, laugh, and focus on target and being smooth on the next shot. This is golf, not rocket science. You are going to miss more shots than you are going to hit. Don't worry about it.

Relax, pick a target, swing smoothly.

After that, try a few fairway woods, then grab the big wood, the driver, which is more than likely made out of metal these days, but they still call it "The Big Stick."

This is, most likely, the club you will hold in your hands on the first tee.

Don't think about it.

Just pick a target and have at it. There just ain't nothing more fun than powering drivers on a driving range, swinging away at a fairway in front of you so wide they could put the entire O'Hare airport on it. And no matter how bad you hit these drivers, you don't have to chase the ball. You just tee another ball up and hit again.

Happy, happy, joy, joy.

You're warmed up, you're swinging smoothly.

Go for the fence. On the range, you have nothing to lose.

5

HELP! WHAT CLUB SHOULD I HIT LAST ON THE DRIVING RANGE?

OKAY, TO BE HONEST, the jury is out on this question.

If the first club you're going to hit on the first hole is a driver, many professionals think that a driver should be your last memory on a driving range, so that when you get to the first tee, you can bring back that fresh memory and repeat.

How does this line of thinking work? Actually, fairly logically, and you're going to use this when you get to the first tee, so pay attention.

While on the range, swinging away with your driver, you are bound to hit one perfect shot, a ball that feels sharp and hard on the club face, that flies straight at your target like you've been playing the game for a hundred years. When that happens, stand there and remember, no memorize the feeling of the swing, watch the ball fly away, and then land. Hold your follow-through like you're posing for a picture done by a guy who hasn't yet figured out his new camera.

Memorize the feel of the shot.

Put the image of the shot in your mind's eye.

Then put the club away in your bag. Don't try to repeat that perfection until you get to the first tee. All you'll do is screw it up and confuse the issue.

The other side of the argument for which club to hit last votes for one of your wedges. Many professionals think a cool-down is needed in a pre-round practice session. They believe a player should work back from a driver down to a wedge, then a half wedge, then a few chip shots off the end of the driving range tee after that perfect drive.

This thinking assumes a few things. First, you are at a country club that furnishes unlimited practice balls. Or you bought a really big bucket of balls. If you bought the small bucket, make the good driver your last shot, even if that perfect last shot is three balls from your last ball. Hit the good shot, stop, and walk away.

The second thing cool-down thinking assumes is that you are there on the range far enough ahead of your tee time to take the extra time. Make sure you save some time for putting, remember.

So, let's assume you have the range balls and the time, why not work back down the clubs? It only seems like a logical way to practice. And what can hitting a few more golf balls hurt?

Again, let me repeat. While you are doing this, focus on targets and swinging smoothly.

So, to answer the question of this chapter, always end with a driver on a great shot if you bought a small bucket.

Or with a big bucket of balls, end chipping a dozen or so balls twenty yards off the end of the tee, but do that only after you have ended the practice with the driver with that perfect shot. Either choice is right, either will work, both make you look like you know what you are doing.

And more importantly, both will help you in different ways get off that first tee with success.

6

HELP! HOW MANY PRACTICE PUTTS IS TOO MANY?

THE ANSWER TO this question is very, very simple. You have hit too many practice putts when you are suddenly late for your tee time and have to rush to the first tee, thus causing you to be upset and likely miss the first shot.

Otherwise, a golfer can never practice putting enough.

Ever.

Let me add some personal comments here.

I used to be a really great putter back when I was young and had a lifetime of extra time. I wasn't that strong from tee to green, but get me on the green and I had a belief that I could make any putt from any distance.

And I often did.

How did I get like that? Simple, actually. I spent hours and hours and hours, day after day, year after year, on putting greens.

I would bet my friends ten cents a hole on a putting contest around the eighteen holes on the putting green. (Later that became a buck a hole, and more even later when I turned professional, but I won't go into that aspect of the game here.)

I even have many memories back in high school of starting my parent's car, aiming the headlights at the putting green, and practicing until after midnight. Of course, back then I needed a real life, and a few more dates, but not having a social life sure helped my putting.

The upshot was that when I got to the golf course and stood over a putt, I never thought of the mechanical movement of putting, I simply just knew the ball was going into the hole because I had made a thousand putts just like the one I had in front of me. And if the ball didn't go in, chances are I just read the break in the green wrong.

This kind of practice needs to be done long before you get to a country club for a big match like we're talking about here. The goal of practice putting when you are at a country club isn't to make your putting better, it's to get the "feel" of the greens.

How fast are they?

How slow?

Do they have grain? (Which way the grass grows because if you can see which way the grass is growing, putts break more that way and less against the grain. Bet you always wondered what those announcers were talking about when they said, "The grain got him.")

So, to be deadly honest, there is no amount of putts on a practice green right before a big match that are going to help you that day. Your putting is either going to suck or be great, depending on a few factors that have nothing to do with the amount of putts you hit before the round.

First, it depends on how much you have practiced your putting at home, on your home course, in your office, or in long hallways when staying at a hotel.

Second, how good you are feeling that day.

Third, and never forget third: Luck. Often great putting is just some luck.

So, before you start the round, just get the feel of the green, the sense of the speed, the look of the hole by hitting a few dozen putts from different distances, then give it up, head back to your cart, and go grab a snack and a bottle of water while you wait to call your group to the first tee.

But, one final tip. Always end your practice putts on a putt you made. Just like the great driver on the green, it will put a positive image of the ball going into the hole in your mind.

Everything about golf is a mind game, so don't fight it.

Just play along.

7

HELP! THE STARTER HAS JUST CALLED OUR GROUP AND I'M FROZEN STIFF

METAPHORICALLY, OF COURSE. Actually, more than likely, you have already shed your morning coat and are down to just a sweater and your golf attire. But that echoing call over the practice putting green sends a wave of excitement and fear through you.

"Smith foursome on the tee, Jones group on deck."

You jump in your cart and follow the small signs toward the first tee. Interestingly enough, on many of these big courses, the first tee is a good distance away. Don't get lost. Trust the signs. They will be much bigger than those warning you away from the dining room in the clubhouse.

A man or woman with a big smile, scorecards, and a quick lecture on the day's local rules will greet you at the first tee. Pay attention to those rules as well, since they may mean the difference between a good day and a bad one. And hope it isn't a "path only" day. If it is, that means you have to leave the golf cart on the path no matter where your shot ends up. By the sixteenth hole on days like that, you tend to aim toward the side of the fairway with the golf cart path. Trust me, it can be a long, long walk from a cart on one side of the fairway to deep in the desert or trees on the other side. Especially if you get to your ball and discover you need a different club.

But assume it's a great day, you can take the cart anywhere, and the local rules are about things like not damaging any cactus.

So how do you make yourself relax enough to hit the ball somewhere down the first fairway? The answer is, simply, you won't relax. But that doesn't mean you can't hit a great shot.

Joke with your playing partners, and make sure you get enough strokes on the bets. I used to make sure I didn't get enough strokes from better players for two reasons. First, it made me play better, or so I thought. Second, I had more money then sense.

Don't do as I did on this topic of setting bets on the first tee. Get the strokes. As far as your friends are concerned, on the bets for drinks and dinner, you are the worst player to ever walk on a golf course and it still wouldn't be fair if they gave you a stroke a hole to make up for your defects.

Of course, they're going to be trying to get the best deal as well, so the compromise ends up taking some first tee time.

When that's all done, and the starter says, "Play away, folks," it's again time to get serious.

Remember that great last drive on the range? Remember how it felt? Now's the time to start thinking about it.

Then follow the very easy steps in the next part that will help you stay calm enough to make contact with the ball and get started into a fun day of golf. Note, I didn't say stay calm completely. I'm not a miracle worker here.

But if you do remember that great shot on the driving range where your drive sailed perfectly on target, you have managed step one.

8

EASING THE TENSION

FIRST, TAKE A DEEP BREATH. Giving birth to this first round isn't going to be as painful as delivering a baby, but breathing really does help if you don't want it to be as messy. The last thing you need to be is light-headed walking up there between the tee markers. Fainting on your golf ball really is the stuff of jokes and legends, although I will have to admit, I have only heard of golfers passing out on the first tee, and one guy going to his knees with a heart attack. I have never actually seen it happen.

And thankfully, it hasn't happened to me.

But it does happen. I thought I might pass out once on the first tee at Olympic Club outside of San Francisco. They had the tee markers backed up so close to a giant window in the old clubhouse, I swore my back-swing was going to break the window between me and a hundred or so people in the bar. The fairway snaked down the hill away from me, with trees on the edge so tall, it looked like I was staring down a tunnel instead of a fairway. I managed to keep breathing, but I have no memory of where that drive went. I do remember sort of coming to as I walked past the woman's tee markers.

So breathe, slowly and deeply while you do the second step, which is to get your driver out of your bag. Toss the head-cover either into the cart's basket behind the clubs, or on the seat of your cart where you will see it when you go to sit down.

Don't take it onto the tee with you. Doing so is just asking for trouble and having to drive back down the first fairway to get it after you remember where you left it. So leave it where you are going to sit on it, or put it in the basket where it can just ride along until you come to your senses.

Third step, no matter how many jokes are flying among your friends and the starter, remember to get your golf ball. I can't tell you how many times it was my turn to go to the first tee and I didn't have a ball ready. For some reason, for some of us, that little fact just slips our minds in this preparation routine.

Breathe.

Get your ball, and put a second one in your pocket just in case. Don't think about why. Just put it there and forget it.

Breathe.

I said don't think about why that second ball is with you. So stop it and breathe.

Now, get at least two tees, one for the ball in your hand, one for a spare in your pocket.

Breathe.

You're ready, so climb onto the first tee.

It doesn't matter if it's flat from the cart path to the tee, or downhill. It's still climbing onto the tee like a prizefighter climbs into a ring in a fight. This is the area you're going to battle.

This is the start of the round.

It's you against yourself and the acreage stretched out in front of you.

Gaze down the fairway at your opponent.

Yeah, I know, it looks impossibly narrow.

And really nasty.

And those looming sand traps could swallow your entire house and not even burp.

Breathe.

Hitting the fairway doesn't matter. Remember that.

Repeat after me... "Hitting the fairway doesn't matter."

The goal now is to just get off this tee box alive and with some dignity intact.

So, instead of staring at the fairway of doom, spend this moment picking a target, more than likely a tree or cactus or rock on a mountain in the distance.

Don't look at those traps unless you are using the edge of a distant one as a target. Just pick a target and ignore the rest of the fairway. Ignore the trees, ignore the deep rough and all the problems that lurk on both sides of the fairway. Just like on the driving range, you're going to put a slow, paced swing on your ball and watch it sail toward your target just like it did on the range.

Got that?

Target. Critical.

Don't think about the problems ahead or the width of the fairway. Chances are, the landing area is much, much wider than it looks anyway. The evil golf course designers can do amazing things with perspectives and visual distractions on golf courses. Ignore them. Don't let those pencil pushers beat you.

Pick a target and nothing else matters.

Now, let me end this chapter with a little story about a first tee.

I wasn't playing, so I was very calm and clear-headed when this all happened.

A Little Side Story

I WAS THE STARTER for all the "rabbits" on the PGA Tour in the winter of 1973 in Palm Springs, California. Back then, they didn't have tour schools or anything else like that. You could play on a PGA Tour event by simply signing up for a Monday morning qualifier and scoring well enough to get one of the top spots that day, which allowed you to play in the tournament.

In 1973, the Monday qualifier for the Bob Hope Desert Classic was at a club called Westward Ho Country Club. I was the assistant professional there under an old-time pro named Zell Eaton. So my job was to sit on the first tee box, check in the young professional players and when the group in front of them was clear, say, "Play away, gentlemen."

Now, understand, in my entire life up to that point, I had never seen such a large bunch of idiots trying to play a game that takes thinking and brains to play well. The first hole that year at Westward Ho Country Club was about 320 yards long, with the last 100 yards of the fairway in front of the green being no more than about ten paces wide between an out-of-bounds on the left and a lake on the right.

No landing area, lots of punishment for anything but a perfect shot.

And no reward for hitting a perfect shot, either.

Any smart person would take one look at the maps we gave them, the yardage booklet, and simply hit a three iron back into the wide part of the fairway, where there was no lake or out of bounds, then take a wedge into the green. Safe. That kind of play made the hole an easy birdie hole.

But safe and smart didn't seem to be words these want-to-be touring professionals had in their vocabulary. Man after man stood up there with driver and either hit it out of bounds or into the water. At least nine out of ten of them.

I was stunned and I learned a great lesson from that day as well. When you are standing on every tee box, pay attention to the hole in front of you for a moment. If there is a lake out there in the middle of the fairway about 200 yards, don't hit your driver.

Again, golf is a mental game. And sometimes that means you have to actually think and plan how to play a hole. Startling concept, I know, but something to think about.

However, I must admit, in my later days of playing the game, I tended to forget this basic rule as well, as many of my golfing friends will tell you in stupidly funny stories.

So, look at the hole. If the driver is still the right play, pick your target. It's almost time.

9

GETTING THE TEE INTO THE GROUND

BACK TO BREATHING.

At this point, this is critical because, as your turn to hit comes and you have to walk forward and put your tee into the ground, you are going to have to bend over. Now breathing and bending over do not go well together. If, for some reason, you don't believe me on this important point, try it at home, next to your bed, with a phone nearby. Hold your breath for as long as you can, then without breathing bend over facing your bed and pretend to put a tee into the carpet.

Make sure you fall onto your bed and not the cat.

Now, imagine falling over your ball, kicking it as you try to get your balance, and landing on the wooden tee marker. Number one, that has got to hurt. Number two, it's just not the way to get a round started.

So, you are fine with the breathing thing, but your hands are shaking. What I'm about to tell you next is critical.

Put the ball on the tee in your hand.

The ball and the tee are now one unit, not to be parted until you force the separation with a mighty swing.

Sure, on television, you see the pros putting the tee in the ground with the ball, then picking up the ball, looking at it, then putting it down on the tee so that the logo on the ball is where they want it to be.

You can do that for the next seventeen holes as well. But for this first hole, just leave the ball and the tee as one unit in your hand.

Then, from about five steps away, pick a spot where you are going to put the tee and ball. There is a critical second point to this. Make sure the spot is behind and between the tee markers. Your golfing buddies and the starter tend to frown on you playing either ahead or outside the markers. And besides, it's against the rules and can cost you strokes.

An aside right here. If you don't own a Rules of Golf book, go buy one and spend a few nights reading it at home. There are other books with examples, written in an interesting manner, to explain each rule, but start with the little Rules of Golf booklet and keep it in your bag.

But at the first tee, the most important rule is to get the ball teed within an imaginary rectangle that has the leading edge between the two tee markers and extends backward two club lengths.

Pick your teeing spot with a couple things in mind.

Is your swing clear of any overhanging tree limbs and too-close benches? And can you stand normally if you put the ball in that one spot, without having to stand straddling one of the tee markers?

On the first tee, it's just safer to pick a spot right square in the middle of the markers, back about two feet. Very safe there.

Now, with your focus on that spot in the grass, and your breathing under control, make the motion of putting the tee in the ground one movement. Don't hesitate, don't get down on one knee, don't bend over like a stork wanting to put your head into the ground. Simply, at the end of a stride, bend forward and just get the teen into the ground, then stand up.

Ninety-nine percent of the time, this will be good enough with standard tees. That one percent of the time the ball falls off, just pick up the tee and the ball again, put them together in your hand, and get them into the ground again.

Then pretend like that never happened. No jokes, nothing. And for heaven's sake, never say that lame sentence, "Well, that's one."

It's not, everyone knows that, so don't say it. Just makes you look like an idiot and no one will laugh.

So, with the ball teed up, you are focused on your target and that's all that matters.

Stop looking at those big fairway bunkers.

Target. Just think target.

You should be like the Dustan Hoffman character in the movie *Little Big Man* right before he fires a gun. Remember how he went "snake-eyed?" Don't go snake-eyed, actually, because you have to still see the ball enough to hit it, but do the same kind of focus on your target as the Hoffman character does.

Nothing else matters but the target.

Block out all other things.

And don't forget to breathe.

Going "snake-eyed" and fainting could really worry your golfing buddies. And might just get you life-flighted to the nearest hospital.

10

TAKING A DEEP BREATH, MAYBE TWO

DON'T SKIP THIS SECTION just because you think I've already pounded the breathing thing home. This is different.

Right now, you have your ball teed up, you've stepped back directly behind the ball, you have your driver in your hand, and you're about to step to the ball and address it.

Your golfing buddies are silent, watching.

The group on deck has arrived and are sitting in the carts, watching.

The starter is watching.

It's the nightmare come to play itself out in real life.

No, not hardly. Not with all the things that have gone right to get you to this point this morning.

So, standing there, staring at your target and nothing else, the ball two steps in front of you, it's time for the final few details of the preparation.

Take two, long, very deep breaths. This will get you enough oxygen to get you through the shot without problems. But two deep breaths like that also relax muscles. It's like a signal to your body to let the stress go.

Just like Jack or Tiger or any of the big guns on the tours, while you are doing these breathing exercises, focus on your target. If you haven't noticed them doing this, watch the next time they show a professional player tee off on television. They are not just staring lamely down the first fairway hoping to have their ball land out there somewhere. No, they are staring intently, snake-eyed at a single target.

And they are taking in and letting out long, deep breaths.

Do the same.

This single-minded focus tends to block out all the problems that could happen as a result of a poor shot. This focus tends to bring in only the aspects of a good shot.

And if you do this focus while taking the two deep breaths, it somehow puts that single focus down into the part of the brain that steers the golf swing. I don't think there have really been studies on why this happens, but trust me again, it does.

And if you don't trust me, pay attention during the next tournament on television, especially to the big ones like the Masters or US Open that show the leaders teeing off on the first tee.

You will see an amazing amount of deep breathing and snake-eyed focus. If the camera angle is good on Tiger on a first tee, you will see him acknowledge the applause when his name is called, then you will see in his eyes that he actually just closes out everything around him but his target. It's an amazing skill to be able to do that. Us mortals can't do that completely, but we must try.

You must try.

Focus on the target and take two deep breaths.

This will take about three seconds. If you take any longer than that, your playing buddies might say something and break the mood.

Besides, you don't want to take any longer than a few seconds standing behind your ball staring forward. There's just too much chance you might freeze up.

So breathe twice, focus on the target, and then step toward the ball.

11

VISUALIZING THE PATH OF THE BALL

YOU'RE STEPPING TOWARD the ball, the target is solid in your mind.

Now, remember that final great shot you made on the driving range?

Remember the feel of it?

Remember how the ball went right toward the target?

That's what you need to be doing now.

Remembering and visualizing how the ball sitting in front of you is going to go sailing toward the target.

Take your quick practice swing, thinking about how that perfect drive on the driving range felt.

But more importantly, that practice swing is done to make sure you have the memory of that good shot in your mind. Look up at your target as you finish the swing.

See it?

See the imaginary ball floating right out there, right at the target?

Okay, okay, don't take very long on this. Maybe a fraction of a second is all. You stand there posing with your practice swing and your golfing buddies will really, really start making jokes.

Nasty jokes, like calling you "poser boy" after David Caruso in that television show *Miami: CSI.* Trust me, if you haven't seen that show, watch it once and you will know exactly why you can only take a few moments on this.

But it doesn't take long to visualize a perfect golf shot, to get the memory back into your mind.

Do it.

Then step to the ball, look once more at your target with the memory of that perfect shot. You are there.

You are ready to start your round.

From bag drop through the golf shop, from driving range to the practice green, through an early morning snack to walking onto the first tee, it has all come to this moment.

You are ready.

For heaven's sake, don't whiff it.

Just kidding.

Take one last deep breath and then...

12

...JUST HIT THE STUPID THING

A COUPLE OF QUICK THINGS for you to do correctly in this fraction of a second you are swinging. And it is amazing how many thoughts can go through a golfer's mind during a swing. Sometimes it feels I could write entire novels in a back-swing.

But one final thought is important, besides visualizing the path of the ball toward your well-focused target.

Keep your attention on the ball.

Actually, keep your direct gaze on a dimple on the back of the ball, and if your eyesight isn't good enough to see a dimple from a standing position, what are you doing on a golf course anyway?

Keep your gaze on that spot until the ball vanishes from your sight and there is nothing but grass. Not one moment earlier.

It will take a fraction of a second after impact for your brain to make note that the ball has vanished, and this will be enough time to allow you to keep your head steady enough to make a good swing.

Why this advice now? Simple. You have intense focus on the target, intense visualization of the path of the ball, intense memory of the good shot on the driving range. Right? All that will make your brain excited to see the outcome of this shot. And thus, you might look up before the swing is finished.

Looking up has the effect of pulling up your shoulders with your head and chin. And when you pull up your shoulders in the middle of your swing, only three ugly things can happen.

One, you manage to make contact and get the ball into the air, but it goes way to the right, way fast.

Second, you make contact with the top of the ball and it does the bounce-bounce thing off the front of the tee box, through the woman's tees, and often doesn't even make it to the mowed part of the fairway.

Or third, you pull your head and shoulders up enough to miss the ball completely.

Whiff.

Nightmare of sweating sheets and laughter from friends.

So, keep your gaze focused intently on the dimple on the back of the ball and then don't look to see where the shot went until the ball has vanished.

Congratulations, you now have made it off the first tee. Go have fun, enjoy the day, beat your friends out of dinner and drinks, and mount the score card on a plaque when you get home.

Then, practice your putting. Your score could have been ten shots lower if you had just made a few more putts.

TRUE STORIES FROM THE FRONT LINES

How I Didn't Play with Bob Hope (and Lived to Tell About it)

March, 1973. Palm Springs, California

I WAS A YOUNG GOLF PROFESSIONAL, just fresh into the big world of golf. I had gotten very, very lucky and had been hired the previous fall as the assistant professional by one of the greats of the game of golf, a top player back in the thirties and early forties named Zell Eaton. In his back office, Zell had framed wonderful newspaper articles about how he won this or that tournament, or how he beat Ben Hogan two up, or how he took Byron Nelson to the last hole before winning in a playoff. I used to love standing in front of that wall of framed awards and articles and just read.

Why such a great of the game picked me, a kid from Idaho, to be his assistant, I'll never know. I was cocky, untrained, and not that good of player compared to what I ended up being a few years later. I thought I was good at the time.

Oh, boy, did I have a lot to learn.

For some reason, Zell decided he was going to teach me. And his lessons didn't just include him sitting patiently in a folding lawn chair on the driving range while I hit thousands of golf balls a day, many of them by the lights of my car after we had closed up the golf shop. He did that, often. But in fact, many of his lessons concerned making sure I knew just how good I was, and how much better others around me were. Those lessons were humbling, to say the least, but they did as Zell figured they would. They made me practice harder and harder. And thus get better and better.

And the harder I practiced, the more I showed the drive to learn, the more he wanted to help me.

One big lesson concerned the fear that this book is talking about. By the spring of 1973, Zell had no doubt that I wanted to be good, that I wanted to learn how to play, but he also had no doubt I had no idea what it was really like to stand on a first tee of a major tournament. Now, understand, I had won my share of amateur tournaments up to this point. He figured, rightfully, that they didn't count.

By that March, I had yet to play as a professional, and Zell figured it would be good for me to start slow. Sort of, anyway. He wanted me to work up to some of the tournaments I planned to play that summer up north.

So start small it would be. No real money on the line. Just a charity fund-raiser for the Heart Fund. The idea the charity had was that one local golf professional and one local celebrity would team with two rich players who had paid a lot of money to the charity to play a round of golf.

So, as our course representative, he sent me. When he told me, I felt bad for the poor rich people who would be stuck playing with a lowly assistant from Westward Ho Country Club.

Zell, in his way, just smiled and said, "Don't worry. They'll get their money's worth."

Somehow, he had arranged for me to play with Bob Hope.

In my very first professional golf tournament.

I didn't know this until I was standing on the practice tee the next morning at Desert Island Country Club.

I didn't pass out when the starter told me who my "local" celebrity would be, but I'm sure it was only the training of making myself breathe that saved me from that fate right there.

Now, a couple of things transpired to change what I visualized was a coming disaster. First off, the starter saw my panic. This was years and years before I developed any kind of poker face. Besides, when he told me, I'm sure I went pure white, then turned shades of gray. It would have been hard to miss.

"Problem?" he asked.

"Just first professional tournament shakes," I said.

The guy laughed and said, "Yeah, Zell told me that was the case. Don't you like Bob Hope?"

I had grown up in Idaho, sitting watching Bob Hope specials on a black-and-white television before color was even thought of. Did I like Bob Hope? How do you answer a question about a god like that?

"I sure do," I think I managed to say. Right at that moment, I was sure I was going to pass out on the first tee and be one of Bob Hope's jokes in his next television special. Or I would throw up and then pass out, making everything so bad, they would do a skit about what happened. A really funny skit.

At that moment, fate decided to take a hand and spare me. A rain drop hit the starter. Rain might have hit me, but trust me, at that moment, in my state of fear and panic, I wouldn't have noticed.

It doesn't rain that often in Palm Springs, but this was still winter, and it was a cold morning.

The starter nodded to me and said, "I'll be right back." Then he headed down the practice tee box where Bob Hope was entertaining about a thousand people that were going to walk with him. That guy could really be funny. A little crude in real life compared to his television specials, but really funny.

I turned back to the remaining practice balls and tried to put two thoughts together. I think the two thoughts were, in this order.

"Oh, my, I'm going to play with Bob Hope."

And then, "Oh, NO! I'm going to play golf with Bob Hope."

I am sure I repeated that sequence of thoughts through about twenty practice balls.

I went to taking deep breaths trying to calm down, but all I could think about was that first tee and whiffing that first shot and then passing out. I was having that nightmare back then and at that moment it seemed very real and very possible.

It started to rain even harder, and Bob Hope and most of the crowd at the other end of the practice tee headed for the club house, just leaving a few of us on the tee box.

I started hitting some easy shots, taking deep breaths and forcing myself to calm down. I could do this.

Zell wouldn't have put me in this situation if he didn't think I could do it.

Bob Hope was only a man. I could play with him.

It started raining harder, so I got out my rain gear and kept hitting balls. Rain would help. Slick grips are always a great excuse for missing a shot.

Then they called the group ahead of us to the tee.

I hadn't even hit a putt yet, so I made one slow, smooth swing, as Zell had been teaching me to do all winter, then headed for the practice green beside the first tee.

As I reached there, the starter came out of the club house and walked up to me. I remember his words well.

"Bob's decided to wait out the rain and maybe just play nine. You want to tee it up with McLean Stevenson instead?"

Lt. Col. Henry Blake of *M.A.S.H.* One of my favorite characters on one of my favorite shows.

I think I nodded. But at that moment, I was so relieved to not have to play with Bob Hope, the starter could have told me I was playing with the President of the United States and I would have been happier.

"Great," the starter said. "You're up next."

I ended up riding in the cart with McLean. He was as funny and as nice in real life as he seemed on television. And we had a blast.

And I hit my drive perfect off the first tee.

But the story doesn't end happily right there.

By the seventeenth hole, the weather had cleared and I was really enjoying the day. I also had it two under par with only the last hole to play. Bob Hope's crowd had gone out on the back nine ahead of us, and not more than a few dozen people had followed us around, with McLean entertaining them.

At that time, the last hole of Desert Island Country Club was a fairly short par four, with water all the way along the left side. I hit a perfect drive and was within an easy wedge from the green, over a finger of water to a mostly island green.

Not a problem. I hit a perfect second shot that I remember McLean cheered for while the ball was in the air, telling it to go in the hole.

The shot looked that good.

The ball hit about ten feet short of the pin, bounced once toward the hole, then spun back and kept rolling all the way back down into the water.

The twenty or so people around the green moaned so loudly, I could hear them across the water.

You think that kind of thing doesn't happen? Watch the Master's Golf Tournament some time.

You can also see this same shot on the golf movie *Tin Cup* where Don Johnson's character hits his shot onto the green on the last hole to have it spin back. Of course, for that silly movie, he was hitting a wood and in those days, you couldn't get a wood to spin backwards if your life depended on it.

In real life, with McLean Stevenson sitting in the cart, I hit a perfect wedge and it spun back.

McLean tossed me another ball from my stash in the cart as I laughed. He made a joke which was actually funny and relaxed me. At that point, it didn't much matter. I had survived the day.

So I dropped another ball over my shoulder (as the rules said we had to do in those days) and hit another perfect wedge. The ball mark was about ten inches beyond the first ball mark in the green, right in front of the hole.

The ball hit, bounced once, then spun back into the water.

It looked exactly like the first shot.

Now I'm really laughing because those two shots were so perfect, but as can happen in golf, the end result really sucked at the same moment.

The groan got louder from around the green.

"I think you need more club," McLean said to me, laughing. He tossed me another ball out of the cart, I dropped it, and hit a shot that McLean again said was perfect.

The ball hit six feet short of the pin, just two strides away, bounced forward so close to the pin that people around the green shouted for it to go in the hole.

Yeah, right. Only in the movies. My shot, with an amazing amount of spin, took off for the front of the green like it wanted to come back to the cart. It hit the water so hard, I thought it might actually skip like a stone.

The moans got really loud at that point.

McLean fell out of the cart laughing.

I kid you not. He was a pretty good and very avid golfer in his day, and he knew just how insane this was. And how good the shots were I had hit.

I knew how insane this was.

Now we both had the giggles.

A young golf professional and a seasoned actor giggling in the middle of a fairway. Not a pretty sight, I can tell you.

Go ahead, try hitting a golf ball with someone like McLean Stevenson making jokes and giggling. It was damn near impossible, but after a few minutes, I finally stopped laughing long enough to make a swing.

The next shot, as you might imagine it would, sailed clear over the green and the only thing that stopped it from going in the water behind the green was a bunker. I blasted out and made a decent putt for a ten on the hole.

I got cheers from everyone watching and McLean bought me a drink in the bar where Bob Hope was telling jokes to friends.

I went from two under to four over in one hole, and didn't care. I had played one of the most enjoyable rounds of my life with a wonderful man and a great actor.

And I didn't end up playing with Bob Hope.

The next day, on the range, Zell Eaton spent two hours teaching me how to hit a wedge shot without spin. I just wish he had gotten to that shot a few days earlier in the lesson plan.

My Best and Worst Tee Shot Ever Was the Same Shot

BACK UP in time a little to the fall of 1972. Palm Springs, California.

I was a young golf professional, just starting to be taught how to really play the game by Zell Eaton. I was also struggling to make ends meet, since I had no real money when I got the job with Zell.

My best friend, Jim Kiser, had helped me get from Idaho to Palm Springs and get set up for the job in an apartment. Jim was a college student at the time, headed to a great career in law, and he was a fine golfer. Just don't tell him I told you.

In Palm Springs during those days was a par three golf course, called an "executive course" for reasons lost in time. I have no memory of the name of the place, and I know it doesn't still exist, long ago replaced by an expansive big course and expensive homes. But in 1972, this big square piece of desert had been turned into a dry, hard golf course, fenced in from the tumbleweeds and blowing sand.

And it had one feature that got it a lot of play.

It had lights.

And it stayed open on some nights far past midnight.

For a young, avid golfer like I was at the time, this was heaven. A place to go to practice my short game until all hours of the morning. Needless to say, I spent a lot of time on those dry, dusty fairways and small, hard greens.

One night, my friend Jim, before heading back north to school, decided to go along and play a round with me. We were somewhere on the back nine, facing a hole about 120 yards long, which was fairly long for that course. It was past eleven in the evening, but we were young, strong, and had nothing better to do.

If I remember right, Jim teed off first and missed the green to the right.

I stood up there, and with the swing that Zell Eaton hoped to make worthwhile, tried to hit an easy wedge, planning to make the ball land short and bounce up onto the hard green.

To say I missed the shot would be a very large understatement.

I bladed it, which means the leading edge of the club cut into the ball like a knife.

The ball bounced once or twice just getting off the tee, hit something off to the left of the hole, while bouncing, and then just kept bouncing.

And bouncing.

And bouncing.

First right, then left, then back right toward the green.

I think there had to be a hundred gopher holes out there in that rough for the ball to do that.

It was still bouncing and moving at a pretty good speed when it reached the green, slammed into the pin, and dropped into the hole.

Hole-in-one.

The only perfect shot in golf.

I had been playing for almost twenty years at that point, and that was my first hole-in-one.

I have played for decades since, and that is still my only hole-in-one.

Witnessed by Jim.

Near midnight.

On a course that no longer exists.

I don't often talk about the shot, to be honest.

But it did teach me a lesson that I never forgot. The only thing that really matters is the score on the card.

I was watching Arnold Palmer play a few holes at Indian Wells Country Club later that winter in the Bob Hope Desert Classic. On one hole, the first hole where I joined his "Arnie's Army" gallery, he duck-hooked his drive. It would have hit a home and gone out-of-bounds if it hadn't hit a palm tree instead.

Standing under the palm tree, he rolled his next shot across the fairway. The ball bounced off the brick side of a house, and barely got back in bounds in the rough.

I had watched him for exactly two shots and all I could see was a real hack of a player. He then hit a really nasty shot that barely got off the ground and just sort of rolled up onto the front edge of the green of the short par four.

I had now watched three shots and Arnie had hacked all three of them.

Then he stood up there and made the putt and walked off with a par.

And the lesson of my hole-in-one earlier was again pounded home.

It doesn't matter how pretty, how ugly, or how just plain lucky a shot is, what counts is the final score on the card.

But, that said, I sure hope your holes-in-one are a little more attractive than mine was.

And maybe at a better time of day.

Fear and the Art of Putting from the Middle of the Fairway

FAST FORWARD A FEW YEARS from those first two stories. For me, it's now the summer of 1976 in Northern Idaho. I am a second-year architecture student in the little town called Moscow, the home of the University of Idaho. I still loved golf, but I had decided I hated traveling as much as it took to be a rabbit on the professional tour during those days.

You don't think that's a good reason to stop working toward something you love? Trust me, just spend a few months alone in a hotel room, with nothing to think about but golf, nothing to look forward to but more and more weeks in hotel rooms. And I was good. Darned good, after the years with Zell, so I could see making it on the tour and maybe doing nothing but spending the rest of my life in hotel rooms.

You think touring professionals have it easy, think again. It's a hard, nasty life out there on the road, and it takes a real special kind of person to do it. I clearly liked books, reading, and other things far more than I liked living out of the trunk of my car.

So one fine day, while I was the head professional of my own course in Palm Springs, getting ready to go play some mini-tours or maybe some stops on the Canadian Tour, I got thinking about the long road ahead. And the linked hotel rooms, year-after-year, and the thought just made me shudder.

I just quit, sold everything, and went back to finish a college degree I had started in the late sixties.

So, when I got to college, what did I decide would be a good job for me while attending college? Golf Professional, of course. I seemed to have a little experience at it at that time. So the nice head professional at the Elks Golf and Country Club hired me to be his assistant, starting in the early spring, through the summer, and ending early fall. And he promised he would work with my school schedule.

He also wanted me to play in tournaments, both as a professional in regional events representing the course, and as the club pro going with members to tournaments called pro-ams.

I agreed. At the time, after a long winter of doing nothing but studying, it sounded like fun.

But during the years since I had first turned professional, and that spring of 1976, the PGA had changed some rules for its members. One of the rules they added was a playing test. In other words, you had to be good enough playing the game before they would let you into their tournaments.

I heard that and just laughed, if I remember right. Good enough to the PGA during those days was something like playing 36 holes of golf in less than ten over par. My thinking was I could do that in my sleep.

One cold March day in the spring of 1976, the section of the PGA decided to test its young professionals.

The test course was a very easy golf course in Spokane, Washington that sat on a bluff overlooking a river. That Monday morning, twenty-eight of the Pacific Northwest Section's PGA young golfers gathered, including me.

I had skipped a few classes to be there, got up at three in the morning to make the drive, and hadn't even touched my golf clubs for six months of a long Northern Idaho winter. But I had no worries at all that I would pass the silly test. My memories of the lessons from Zell just years before were still fresh, and during my last days of working full time in the game of golf, I seldom had a round of golf near par, let alone over par.

Ten over par in thirty six holes would be a joke.

The joke was on me.

None of us made it.

Not one of us.

I was fifteen over, low score out of all of us, and felt darned happy about that score. The wind was blowing at a constant thirty miles per hour, the rain couldn't decide if it wanted to be sleet or snow. And it never let up. Not for one minute. It was the longest, most miserable day in my golfing life.

We all figured the PGA section would adjust the test for the conditions of the day, but nope, ten over was the score and that was that.

They did, however, quickly decide to schedule another test because no PGA section up to that point had had everyone fail.

Not one assistant in all the Pacific Northwest and a few head pros taking the test could play in a tournament and that was the last thing any section of the PGA needed at that point in publicity. So the retake of the test would be on the same course in two weeks.

By the time I had made the two-hour drive back to Moscow, I was so angry, I could have bitten through the shaft of my driver. I could just hear Zell's voice in my head.

"Conditions don't matter. Only the score matters."

And in this case, I had failed. Sure, I had the best score of anyone there that day, but so what? I had made more mistakes than I could ever imagine, including the big one of going in unprepared and not thinking correctly about the goal ahead.

Now understand, I was still very cocky about golf, and I hadn't failed a test in golf in a long, long time. I wouldn't fail a second time.

Every day, between classes, snow, wind, or rain, I went out to the course and hit golf balls, practiced putting, worked the winter kinks out of the Palm Springs golf swing.

By the time that second test came around, I was behind in school and mad about that.

And really, really mad I had failed the qualifier the first time.

I went up to Spokane the night before this time and stayed in a hotel to get the rest needed for the next day's 36 holes of play. I worked over the map of the course, planning a game plan, making notes as to which holes to play safe, which holes to attack.

In other words, I did the same thing I used to do for golf tournaments before going back to school.

The morning of the second test broke clear and cold. The weather this time would not be much of a factor.

By the time I had made it through my warm-up routine on the range and putting green, I was even angrier that I was even there. I was in the third group to tee off. All I remember on that first shot was that I swung as hard as I could because there was just no trouble on either side of the fairway to get into. Turned out, I hit one of the longest drives of the day there among all the professionals.

I birdied the first hole with a tap-in putt.

I birdied the second hole with a three foot putt.

I chipped in for an eagle on the par five third hole.

I birdied the fourth hole with a ten foot putt.

Five shots under par in four holes.

Now that was the player I remembered myself being from Palm Springs. Zell would have been proud of me.

But what now?

I knew I couldn't keep playing out of the anger. I had to play smart, stay focused on the only reason I was there, which was to pass the stupid ten-over-par test.

So, on the tee of the fifth hole, I changed style. From that moment on, I played safe. I had 32 holes left to play and fifteen shots over par to spend to make the test score.

I made pars on the rest of the holes on the first nine, for a 30 on the par 35, rimming out a birdie putt on the 9th hole for what would have been only 29 in my life.

I was two over par on the next nine. Still three under for the first eighteen holes.

Two over par on the next nine, playing safe all the way.

Then, still even par for the tournament since my little splash of birdies right off, I came to the really nasty sixteenth hole of the second time around, actually my 33rd hole of play that day.

It was a short par four with out-of-bounds the entire right side of the fairway and out-of-bounds about ten feet behind the green. I had already played it once and it was one of the holes I had worked out the night before that was a real danger to a score.

"Play safe. Stay away from that out-of-bounds."

I remember thinking that as I stood on that tee.

So, much to the laughter of the rest of the pros in my group, I turned and aimed my drive over the bench and clear out into the bordering fairway. In fact, I hit it so far in that direction, I hit it clear across the neighboring fairway and into the rough on the other side.

Safe.

The rest of my group sort of waved goodbye to me as they started down the hole we were playing and I started off at an angle.

My second shot now had another problem. Instead of just having the out-of-bounds on the right and behind the green, I was so far left, I had to aim directly at the out-of-bounds just to aim at the green.

And the green sloped off the back toward that out-of-bounds behind it.

All I could think about was bouncing my shot out of the rough over the green and then standing there in a neighboring fairway and doing what I called a "McLean Stevenson" meaning a replay of that ten I took in Palm Springs in my first professional tournament.

So I played safe with my second shot, took a good two clubs too little for the distance, and aimed my shot toward the front of the green, into a wide spot in the fairway. My plan was that I could then chip up and make the putt for another par. I had learned the lesson well of it didn't matter how, it was just how many that counted.

My ball stopped in front of the green, a good fifty paces short.

As I stood over the third shot, all I could think about was blading the ball over the green and out-of-bounds. I just couldn't shake that nasty thought, which meant more than likely, that was exactly what was going to happen.

I stepped back and looked at the situation. I only had two holes to play after this. What difference would a bogey make at this point? I was still even par and the cut line was ten over. Bogey didn't matter, but numbers higher than that did.

So I put my wedge back into my bag and took out the club I had the most confidence with. My putter.

Now, understand, there was a good fifty paces to the front of the green, and another twenty paces to the pin. All downhill. All over rough, late-winter ground.

In other words, I had no idea where this ball was going to go. The correct shot was to chip it into the air.

I didn't care what was correct.

At that moment, I just wanted to bang my ball down by the green, maybe on the front edge, two putt and go to the next hole.

The other three professionals started laughing at my club choice as I walked up to the front of the green to get a sense of the distance. But they had no right to laugh and they knew it. I was a good six shots ahead of my nearest playing companion. I just wanted to get off this stupid golf course and get home to see how far behind I was with my classes.

So, pretending I was standing on a really, really big green with a really, really long putt, I hit the shot.

I remember my ball bounced a good ten feet into the air fairly soon after I hit it.

Putts aren't supposed to bounce like that.

Then still bouncing, my ball kept rolling and bouncing, right onto the front of the green.

Then it broke right, then broke back left, hit the pin, and went into the hole.

Birdie three on the scorecard.

It wasn't pretty, it wasn't done by the book, and the entire hole was played out of sheer fear and common sense.

And it sure was fun.

I passed the test with a par-par finish on the last two holes. Actually, I was eight shots ahead of the second-place finisher.

That summer, due to summer school classes, I ended up never playing in any other tournaments. The following year I didn't renew my PGA membership status and a few years later I applied to the USGA and got my amateur standing back. That was my last tournament as a professional golfer.

But that hole was a way for me to see everything Zell had taught me and what I hope many will get from this book. Fear is a part of the game of golf, as well as in life. Learn how to play with fear, and how to use it.

Don't panic.

Just learn the routines, keep your head and wits about you, keep your breathing regular, and think.

And always remember, it doesn't matter how pretty a golf shot is. All that matters is the final score.

That, and having a great time.

ABOUT THE AUTHOR

USA Today bestselling writer Dean Wesley Smith published more than a hundred novels in thirty years and hundreds of short stories across many genres.

He wrote a couple dozen *Star Trek* novels, the only two original *Men in Black* novels, Spider-Man and X-Men novels, plus novels set in gaming and television worlds. He wrote novels under dozens of pen names in the worlds of comic books and movies, including novelizations of a dozen films, from *The Final Fantasy* to *Steel* to *Rundown.*

He now writes his own original fiction under just the one name, Dean Wesley Smith. In addition to his upcoming novel releases, his monthly magazine called *Smith's Monthly* premiered October 1, 2013, filled entirely with his original novels and stories.

Dean also worked as an editor and publisher, first at Pulphouse Publishing, then for *VB Tech Journal,* then for Pocket Books. He now plays a role as an executive editor for the original anthology series *Fiction River.*

For more information go to www.deanwesleysmith.com, www.smithsmonthly.com or www.fictionriver.com.

Want to read more by Dean Wesley Smith?
Try his Poker Boy series, including the first novel,
The Slots of Saturn, on sale June 2014.

www.ingramcontent.com/pod-product-compliance
Lightning Source LLC
Chambersburg PA
CBHW031525040426
42445CB00009B/394

* 9 7 8 0 6 1 5 9 3 5 2 9 4 *